LORD OF
OUR JOURNEY

LORD OF
OUR JOURNEY

DERICK BINGHAM

Ambassador

Lord Of Our Journey

AMBASSADOR PRODUCTIONS LTD
Providence House
Hillview Avenue
Belfast BT5 6JR, UK.

ISBN   0 907927 53 X

Also distributed by
Highway Publishing
Unit One Cofton Road,
Marsh Barton
Exeter EX2 8RD, UK.

Printed in the United Kingdom by Ambassador Productions Ltd.

Contents

	Introduction	7
1	Broad But Not Deep	9
2	Camping With God	12
3	Satan's Strategy	15
4	I Count You Rich	18
5	God's Giants Are Weak Men	21
6	The Unanswered Question	24
7	Best Is Yet To Be	27
8	A Dove In A Crow's Nest	30
9	Keep Your First Love	34
10	Trial By Fire	37
11	Have A Talk With Yourself	41
12	Do You Ever Doubt?	45
13	The Interrupted Prayer	48
14	Forgiveness Puts The Singing Back	52
15	Christ's Heartbeat	55
16	You Are Invited To A Banquet	58
17	Pie In The Sky	62
18	A Cool Hand On A Hot Head	65
19	A Lick Of Paint	69
20	Buy Some Friends	73
21	The Devil Has No Truce	77
22	Silent Planet	81
23	Please Make My Brown Eyes Blue	85
24	Sowing Is Painful	89
25	Come Out Of The Prison	92
26	The Heart-Stealer	95

Introduction

Recently I went around the world. It was not in an ocean going ship-of-the-line with bully beef every three hours and a full year or two passing before I got there. The food was delectable and it took, in all, only a few days to travel right around the globe.

The thing that impressed me, though, was the fact that the number of miles from my destination kept coming up on a screen at the front of the aircraft. Distances from places of interest were there too. "Tahiti; 500 miles", it read or "Java; 1,000 miles". It was fascinating.

For the christian, life is a journey. There is a point to it all. Life is not an aimless moving from nowhere to nowhere. Recently, the brilliant Shakespearian actor Kenneth Branagh said, "I hate the church ... I hate organised religion". Now, on the face of it, you would think a chap like that would never think about destination. Don't you believe it. In the very same interview with "The Times" he said, "When you are busy you are avoiding all the old larger questions. But they come and haunt you whether you like it or not. You are suddenly faced with all the old cobblers about "Who am I and what am I doing here and of course in my case that something dreadful is going to happen". It is not just folk who go to churches who think about the purpose of life and the ultimate destination of the human soul. As King Solomon once said "Eternity is in everybody's heart".

On the journey of life I often ease the pace with the joy of painting in water colour (hence at the request of my publisher, the cover of this book) but even as I paint ships, or the countryside or a poppy in a windowbox I am aware that life is transient. Just try and capture in paint the colour of the sky on any afternoon. It passes so quickly.

With all my heart I agree with Prince Charles in his new and most stimulating book "A Vision of Britain" when he says that we seem to have got to a place where man "Glorifies the triumph of science and man's domination over nature. All this", he says, "coincides with what can only be described as the denial of God's place in the scheme of things and the substitution of man's infallibility". He quotes the famous words of Christ who said "What shall it profit a man if he shall gain the whole world and lose his own soul?" The answer is, of course, nothing.

This little book has to do with the christian journey through life. It aims to help and encourage the believer to stride on despite many discouragements along the way. I pray there will also be help for unbelievers that will draw them to the Lord of the journey and that they too may enter the narrow way that leads to life. There is an easier way but it leads to destruction. It too has a Lord of the journey but he cares not for his sheep. The Lord of the narrow way gave His life for His. That has made all the difference. He takes them to a celestial fold which is beyond my pen's description. Onward!

Derick Bingham.

1

Broad But Not Deep

It is possible to have a lot of friends and yet come to ruin in a crisis. Why? Because a lot of our friendships are too broad and not deep.

We are told in Scripture of the deep friendship between David and Jonathan and that friendship lasted through many a crisis because Jonathan certainly stuck with David much closer than any brother David ever had. Their relationship teaches us a lot about the principles of friendship.

We are not told in Scripture whether Jonathan was a witness to David's great victory over Goliath. We are simply told that as David returned from giant-killing and talked with King Saul. Jonathan found his soul being 'knit' with the soul of David.

When you knit something together it is usually of the same nature and there can be no doubt that David's faith kindled with Jonathan's faith.

Consider the faith of Jonathan's friend. Battles, you know, are won long before they are ever fought. What you are in private you will be in public.

Don't think for a moment, if you are self indulgent, that the great occasion will give you the heroism you never showed in private. The crisis will reveal what you are.

The sleeping disciples couldn't watch with Christ for one hour and they were shown up when the crisis hit them a few hours later. They turned and fled.

As Jonathan stood that day looking on David he was not looking on a man of faith who found his faith incompatible with the test of life.

Notice that it was in doing an errand for his father he exercised faith and laid the giant of Philistia low. And remember, he did not neglect one duty for another. Notice that before he left his father's flock he was careful to entrust them to a keeper.

David became the greatest writer of Psalms the world has ever known. He certainly became Israel's greatest king but he certainly didn't believe that you can only do noble deeds when you are delivered from the obligation of family ties.

He did not become faithful in the greater deeds before he was faithful in the least.

David's faith had taken a lot of abuse at home, long before he ever heard the giant mock him. Notice the word 'now' in 1 Samuel 17 v 29. Even Eliab's outburst against David on the eve of his greatest victory brought a gentle answer from the lad.

David showed that day that those who are gentlest under provocation are strongest in the fight.

The faith that so impressed Jonathan had withstood one of the toughest tests of all. It withstood the reasoning of the flesh.

It must have been a sore temptation for David to trust in the reasoning of a carnal, worldly man like Saul. Worldly advice will enmesh you in a life that needs no faith.

If David had not refused Saul's armour he could

never have said to Goliath that *'The Lord saveth not with the sword and spear'*.

David's ability to stand alone by faith in God had a direct link with his ability to enter into a deep friendship with Jonathan. Was it not such an ability that brought Moses from the desert to Pharaoh's palace and his friendship with Joshua?

Was it not such an ability that brought Ruth from obscurity to become such a friend to Naomi?

Was it not such an ability, even when he was a ploughman, that drew Elijah to Elisha?

Was it not such faith in God that made Elizabeth and Mary more than relatives?

Was it not such a faith in the husband and wife team Priscilla and Aquilla that drew Paul and Timothy and Apollos to their home to find not only fellowship but friendship?

Have faith in God, Christian. The result will astound you. You will be able as a result to make deeper friendships than you ever imagined you could. Go on. Have faith in God.

2

Camping With God

I have in my time read interesting language about growing old. The seven ages of man, I have been told, are 'Spills, Drills, Thrills, Ills, Tills, Wills!'.

For me, though, growing older is when you get out of the shower and you are glad the mirror is all fogged up!

Peter wrote about old age, too. He describes his imminent death as *'Knowing that shortly I must put off my tent'*.

It is a very apt description because our bodies are so created by God that they are easily taken down.

Peter describes life as camping (2 Peter 1 v 13) and death is folding up the tent and moving on.

Yet, we need to be persuaded that the eternal world, beyond death, is actually there. Our modern world pours scorn on it, some professed theologians cast doubt upon it. So Peter, teaches that it is based on two vital pieces of evidence.

He says that *'We did not follow cunningly devised fables'* because he saw the glory of the eternal world when Christ was transfigured and he says, *'We have also a more sure word of prophecy ... for the prophecy came not in old time by the will of man: but holy men of God spake as they were moved by the Holy Ghost.'*

In other words, you can trust all that is written in Scripture.

The liberals today tell us they agree that the disciples had a real experience of Christ, but they say that the disciples had great difficulty in trying to get their impressions across. So, they say, the disciples made up stories.

The stories were not real, they were just a way of saying that Jesus was somewhat special. They will tell you that the account of the virgin birth and the resurrection are just stories.

What they say sounds subtly reasonable until you begin to think it through and then it becomes a nightmare. Even more than that, the thing is downright heresy.

They say those things are just an impression, but ask them if they think the impression was exact. Well no, these disciples were just men so you can't trust the impression 100 per cent either! So if we follow them what a pickle we will be in!

How many a young person has listened to the nonsense of the liberals in many a theological college and has got up to preach no longer certain of what he can preach.

They would love to preach the certainty of an eternal kingdom, or the virgin birth, or the transfiguration or the resurrection but they can't actually say these things happened! So they fall to preaching morality and politics.

Peter's view is so different . He says the source of the things he teaches is God. He says the Word of God is utterly reliable.

What is written is not the private interpretation or explanation of it came from God himself.

These Holy men of God spoke and wrote as they were moved by the Holy Spirit.

There is an eternal kingdom because the reliable Word of God says so. This Word is your 'flashlight', (a lamp unto your feet) on the dark path of this life. If you follow it you need never stumble.

You will have it to guide you until *the day dawns and the morning star rises in your hearts*, that is, the Lord himself will come for you.

So Christian, trust God's Word and if you meet a liberal who tells you that Peter is only telling you stories, tell that liberal to set himself up as an apostle if he likes and start a new religion if he wants but please, whatever he does, let him not call it biblical Christianity.

3

Satan's Strategy

Satan is not God. He does not have the essential powers of deity. He does not know as God knows.

He is not everywhere as God is everywhere. he is not all-powerful as God is all-powerful. But one thing is for sure, he has a strategy.

How do we know Satan has a strategy? Speaking through the Letter to the Church at Pergamum the Lord tells the Christians that he knows they are living *'where Satan's throne is'*.

For some strategic reason of his own Satan has 'his seat; at Pergamum. He was not ignorant of the fact that the city was a place of great wealth and fashion.

He set up his throne at the strategic point from which he could best use his influence.

He still does.

The great problem the Christians at Pergamum faced was entering into an alliance with Mammon. Mammon stands for all this world counts great and behind that is the love of money.

Where Mammon reigns you can be sure the devil lurks behind it. Where the excellencies of God's earth create special possibilities for man's abuse, there the devil will set up his throne.

I found this recently while travelling in the beautiful Tayside area of the Scottish highlands. Driving across beautiful glens, by forests teeming with wildlife, one of God's masterpieces of creation, I noticed distillery after distillery built to supply the drink traffic. That beautiful countryside was a source used by Satan for endless misery.

'If you had opened as many people as I have,' said an eminent Ulster surgeon recently, ' and seen what alcohol has done to their livers you wouldn't touch it'. I firmly believe that social drinking even among Christians is leading to serious repercussions.

Recently, an elder of the church with which I had some special services told me how his son had come home drunk one evening. The man remonstrated with his son about his drunkenness and the lad replied, 'But Dad, you bought me my first shandy'.

Do not think ill of me, Christian, because I warn of the great dangers of alcohol. Just remember that one in every three people has the potential to become an alcoholic.

How would you feel if you were the one blamed for introducing a person to alcoholism? Beware of Satan's strategy in this matter.

So it was that where the excellency of God's earth had created special possibilities for man's abuse the devil had set up his throne in Pergamum. The Lord recognised the peril of Pergamum, but very quickly commended the Church for holding fast his name and for not denying *'my faith'*.

Ye he had a complaint about the Church. *'You have there,'* he says, *'some that hold the teaching of Balaam ... you have also some that hold the teaching of the Nicolaitans,'* he adds.

The teaching of Balaam was that since Israel was a covenant people they could safely sin for no harm could happen to them (Numbers 31 v 16). What the teaching of the Nicolaitans was I don't know, but the result was the same as the teaching of Balaam; we know it today as Antinomianism. That is you are safe in your faith - your conduct doesn't matter. It is a terrible heresy.

'Repent,' says Christ, *'To him that overcometh I will give him a white stone'*. What a lovely thought!

The white stone was given to a person justly acquitted after a trial. A white stone was given to a victor returning from a battle.

A white stone was divide in two, between two friends when parting and each would carry with him one half upon which the name of his friend was inscribed. Sometimes, generations later, two men would meet and find they possessed the complementary halves.

So, faithful Christians, you have the white stone of acquittal, of justification, of victory, and of unending friendship. It is true we must abhor false teaching within the borders of our church fellowship, but let us always remember that the test of pure doctrine is purity of conduct.

May you know that balance all your days. That's our strategy and, by the Lord's power, it overcomes Satan's.

4

I Count You Rich

He was just three years old when his father died. His mother took over the family trade and continued the boys' education.

She murdered his stepfather with a dish of poisoned mushrooms. While still young he murdered a teenage boy. At 15 he married but soon had his wife killed. He married again and slew his second wife, too.

In order to marry a third time, he murdered the husband of the women he wanted. He then arranged for his mother's murder, first by guile, unsuccessfully, and then without pretence.

He was an ugly man with a bull neck, bad skin and an offensive odour. At 31 years of age he was sentenced to death by flogging. He fled to a dingy basement and, in the house of a slave, cut his own throat.

He gave the Church of Jesus Christ its first taste of persecution. He was a Roman Caesar. His name was Nero.

The next Caesar, Domitian, was not much better. The blasphemous tyrant gave the Church a second wave of bitter persecution. It was to one of those churches at that time, the Church of Smyrna, that

Christ delivered a letter, recorded for us by John in the Book of Revelation.

The Master addressed the Church speaking of himself as *'The first and the last, who was dead and is alive'*. Those Christians at Smyrna were close to death and their master was identifying closely with them.

Let us always remember that the Lord Jesus is the master of the darker matters, too. He has been to the utmost reaches of death and is alive again.

He has been dead and is alive for evermore. That is a very comforting fact for any church or individual.

I came home from my holidays the other day to find my own city gripped with fear and saw millions of pounds worth of damage done to inner city office property by bomb blast. It would make you weep to see old people killed and youngsters' hope for the future blasted.

I discovered a friend of mine had lost his father-in-law and his mother through illness and death both inside six days.

Another friend of mine had cancer grip his wife and I was praying with him on the phone that he would get a night's sleep.

He described to me the peace that God had given both him and his wife in their deep valley. It was most reassuring. I don't know about you but I am mighty glad that my Lord was dead and is alive for evermore.

When men and women and young people are surrounded by sorrow they are always filled with questioning . It is comforting to know that the Lord Jesus is the answer to those questionings.

'I know', says Christ to the Christians at Smyrna, *'I know your works, and tribulation and poverty'*. Christ speaks from his own experience. He didn't just observe their suffering, he passed through it himself.

19

Is there any greater comfort than the comfort of knowing that your Lord knows what you are passing through? Nothing misses his notice.

He promises that there will be more trouble at Smyrna. *'The devil will cast some of you into prison'*. He says, *'You shall have tribulation ten days; be faithful to death and I will give you a crown of life'*.

The immediate future did not look very bright for them, did it? Yet, suddenly, there is a flash, a gleam of light.

'But you are rich', he says. It seems incredulous. How could they be? What is the Lord saying?

He is saying, 'Smyrna counts you poor but I count you rich. You have been robbed by your persecutors but you have lost nothing.'

They were *'As having nothing, and yet, possessing all things'*. Christ's view of wealth is not the world's view. True Christian wealth never tarnishes, never decays and never fades.

'I'll give you the crown of life', says the Lord. There will come a wealth through suffering for Christ which this world knows nothing of. Are you truly rich, Christian? It is a vital question.

A friend of mine, Heather Skeen and her husband left home and hearth to serve Christ in France recently. Before she left Heather came to say goodbye. *'Some Christians'*, she said with a smile as she was going, *'are so poor, all they have is money!'* Selah.

5

God's Giants Are
Weak Men

A story is told of a British Navy manoeuvre. The signal was given to the convoy of ships to turn 90 degrees. One captain missed the signal and his ship almost collided with the one in front. When in swerved to avoid the crash, the whole convoy was thrown into confusion.

The captain knew he would be in for dismissal so when the Commander signalled to him, 'Captain what are your intentions?' he immediately signalled back, 'Sir, I intend to buy a farm!'

When a great spiritual leader falls disastrously into moral sin, the ramifications are colossal. Even if he who has risen so high for his Lord repents of his sin and admits it, he is faced with overwhelming, gnawing guilt.

Self-loathing fills his heart and people who looked to him for leadership are deeply disappointed. He becomes the sport of the media and the many millions they communicate with.

What would you do with someone God had mightily used if he got involved with a prostitute? You ask his name? His name was Samson. 'Then', says the Bible, 'Went Samson to Gaza, and saw there a harlot, and went in unto her.'

Of course Samson did not only sin at Gaza; soon he was involved with a woman he loved in the Valley of Sorek whose name was Delilah.

Samson toyed and played the fool with Delilah. But soon God withdrew his power from the man. Samson was overwhelmed by his enemies who gouged his eyes out and took him to Gaza to grind at the mill.

What hope was there for this fallen leader of God's people? When thousands of Philistines gathered to sacrifice to their god Dagon and the drink flowed, the cry soon went up, 'We want Samson!'

What fun they had with the sightless fallen Judge of Israel! What degrading things they must have made him do as the laughed and guffawed and made sport.

It was a sad day for the people of God and for their leader.

Do you feel the same about the state of the Church today? Do you feel that moral compromise and desecration of doctrine, selfishness and sheer lack of spirituality are impossible to recover from?

Can we be revived again? The answer is we certainly can.

We read that Samson's 'hair began to grow again'. The emphasis is not so much on what was happening to him naturally as to what was occurring spiritually in his relationship with God.

His growing hair was a visible sign that his fellowship with God was restored and growing.

No matter how far you fall in your spiritual experience, you never fall beyond God's forgiveness. In his weakness Samson began to reach out to the Lord and he was unreservedly forgiven.

But the consequences of his sin were not erased.

Samson grew new hair but he did not receive new eyes. He would never again be able to do what he could have done if he had not sinned, but he was absolutely forgiven and the Lord had a great thing for him to do.

God used Samson's blindness so that the lad who led him round that jeering, drunken, blood thirsting mob could show him where the pillars were in the temple of Dagon.

Crying to God for help, committed to a martyr's death, Samson brought the temple of Dagon crashing down around their heads. His death was a victory over God's people, later to be led to greater heights by King David, had come.

As we look for and long for a spiritual awakening across the world and desire a revival among God's people, we would let the words of J. Hudson Taylor ring in our ears: 'All God's giants have been weak men, who did great things for God because they reckoned on his being with them'.

That's why in Hebrews chapter 11 Samson is called a person of faith. You can be called the same. Go to it!

6

The Unanswered Question

A Bishop was once travelling on a train and a passenger leaned across to him. 'Tell me, Bishop, are you saved?' the passenger asked. The Bishop gently replied, 'In what sense? Do you mean am I saved, am I being saved, or will I yet be saved?'

The Bishop was absolutely right. Salvation is a great Bible word and it has at least three distinct shades of meaning.

Sometimes in Scripture the thought is salvation from the penalty of sin (see Ephesians 2 v 8), sometimes it is salvation from the power of sin when the present tense is used (see 1 Corinthians 1 v 18) and sometimes it is salvation from the very presence of sin itself, namely our being in Heaven - Romans 13 vs 11-12, *'Now is our salvation nearer than when we believed. The night is far spent, the day is at hand.'*

In Hebrews chapter 2 a great question is asked. It is the great unanswered question of the Bible: *'How shall we escape if we neglect so great salvation?'*

As I see it, salvation as mentioned in this vital question is salvation in the sense of salvation from the penalty of sin.

Let's think about such salvation, for it is of paramount importance.

It was a fearful thing in Old Testament days to flout God's law. Soon after the law was given we are told that a man was found gathering sticks on the Sabbath day.

Gathering sticks was innocent enough in itself - but it broke the law of God. They put the man in custody and consulted God as to what should be done to him. God's stern reply was that he should be stoned to death (Numbers 15 vs 32-33).

Now the law of God was 'put into effect' through angels (Acts 7 v 53) and to flout it was fatal, so why should flouting salvation be any less serious? In truth it is even more serious, for salvation 'First began to be spoken by the Lord' and was 'put into effect' by signs and wonders with various miracles, and gifts of the Holy Spirit according to God's own will (Hebrews 2 vs 3-4).

I wonder if there is someone who is reading this column who is neglecting God's offer of salvation in Christ? You might ask, what actually does this salvation offer?

It offers many things but perhaps the greatest is complete and absolute peace with God. A Jew in Old Testament days had to constantly bring sacrifices to the Lord.

As the Priest took those sacrifices and offered them, it was obvious to everyone there were no chairs in his place of service. Why? Because he wasn't allowed to sit down. Why? Because his work was never finished.

But Christ, after he had made one sacrifice for sins forever, sat down on the right hand of God. Why? Because his work of procuring salvation was complete. Wonderful! *It is finished* he cried on the Cross, and died.

To everyone who receives him as Saviour because his work at Calvary was so complete, salvation is given without money and without price.

Peace with God through receiving Christ as Saviour is immediate. Because salvation is free, though, it is not cheap. It cost God Calvary. To neglect it is an eternally fatal thing to do.

'*How shall we escape if we neglect so great salvation?*' says our question. Some people argue that the emphasis is on the word 'we' and that means only converted people. I don't believe them.

The writer to the Hebrews does not take anything for granted. If a person really believes the Lord Jesus you can tell that person they are eternally saved and will never be lost.

The important question is, 'Does that person really believe?' That you can only judge from the evidence and when the evidence is doubtful, the profession is doubtful.

Even though in his heart of hearts the writer believed the people he was writing to were truly saved, he was taking no risk. He was warning them. If they were not truly saved the great danger would be that knowing God's truth they might neglect it and be eternally lost.

So, it is a question which goes out to everyone, everywhere. Let me ask it again to my own generation; '*How shall we escape if we neglect so great salvation?*'

God leaves the question there and so will I.

7

The Best Is Yet To Be

'Stop taking notes,' G. Campbell Morgan used to say to his Bible class, 'I am speculating.' Well, so am I for a moment or two. Ready?

I reckon there are a lot of my readers who have not found it easy to live the Christian life. Many of you have known the jibe of the non-Christian at work, school or college or even in your immediate families.

Some of you may even have forgone marriage because circumstances were such that you could not marry a Christian.

There could be a business man reading this who could have made tens of thousands of pounds on a deal if he had been prepared to give in to bribery and cheating. You refused because you loved the Lord Jesus.

Those who live godly lives always suffer persecution in some form or other and every Christian knows there is a cross to bear if you would follow the Saviour.

In fact our Master warned that those who followed him need not expect softer names or usage than were given to him. We know that and have experienced it but there is one great spur in the midst of it all. That spur is the assurance of seeing his face one day and enjoying heaven with him forever. This is our comfort and the stimulus to patience and endurance.

There is an inheritance before us which is incorruptible and undefiled that will not fade away, reserved in heaven for us (1 Peter 1 v 4). With this in mind, so what if we get snide remarks or suffer job loss or a place at university as thousands of young Christians do at this very moment in some Communist countries?

With such an inheritance to go to, the fact that we will leave no great estate behind us in this world fades into oblivion. As an older friend of mine reminds me when I visit him: 'Cheer up! The best is yet to be!'

But now I want to speculate. What would happen in heaven was not all that was promised? What if it were a disappointment? What if its delights were not a patch on all this world can offer? What then?

The answer is that if that happened God would be ashamed of himself. The Bible emphatically states that it will never happen.

Describing Abraham as being *'Called to go out into a place which he should after receive for an inheritance'* Scripture tells us *'He obeyed ... for he looked for a city which hath foundations, whose builder and maker is God'* (Hebrews 11 v 8 and 10).

The Bible states that God will never be ashamed of his heaven, for, speaking of those who give up things in this world for the Lord's sake it says: *'Truly, if they had been mindful of that country from whence they came out, they might have had opportunity to have returned. But now they desire a better country, that is, a heavenly: wherefore God is not ashamed to be called their God'* (Hebrews 11 v16).

Why does Scripture say this? Because it adds, *'He*

hath prepared for them a city'.

The wonderful truth is that God will have no cause to be ashamed, for all he has promised about that future city will be fulfilled to the exact detail. As far as we will be concerned 'The half will not have been told us'!

Abraham will not have been sorry he left Ur of the Chaldees at God's command, and you, my friend will not be sorry you took up your cross and followed the lovely Lord Jesus through this evil and godless generation.

By God's grace you have been made one of those living stones which have been added to God's spiritual house. Jesus Christ himself is the chief cornerstone.

The promise is that *'He that believeth on him shall not be confounded'*. Think of it! You will not be confounded. The promises will be kept!

It will be the godless who will one day be confounded, they who now appear so smug and self-assured. Their awakening will be fearful; yours will be fantastic!

So, away with the speculation and into certainty. For you, my dear Christian, the best is yet to be!

Though now in your godly living you invite the fury of hell, you have underneath and round about you, the everlasting arms. In such arms you will not be confounded but will be eternally comforted. Cheer up!

8

A Dove In A Crow's Nest

It was Alfred Lord Tennyson who said after a visit to Queen Victoria that 'Up there, in all her glory and splendour, she was lonely'.

Thomas Wolfe, the famous American novelist has said, 'The whole conviction of my life now rests upon the belief that loneliness, far from being a rare and curious phenomenon, peculiar to myself and few other solitary men, is the central and inevitable fact of human existence.'

Wolfe is right and if you could become a really good friend to someone and help them to fulfil all that God wants them to be; wouldn't your life be worth living?

If you never did anything else wouldn't that be an incredibly valuable thing to do? Such friendships are rarely found and are very costly to maintain but have incalculable value. You'll not have many such friendships in your life.

Though rare, such friendships are certainly possible. No matter what age you are, no matter what stage in your career you find yourself, you can be such a friend to someone.

Didn't Moses have Joshua, didn't Daniel have his three friends, didn't Mary of Nazareth have Elizabeth, didn't Peter have John, didn't Paul have Timothy? Didn't the Lord Jesus draw his disciples around him?

It has been well said that 'A faithful friend is a strong shelter; the man who finds one has found a treasure. There is no substitute for a friend and there is no way to measure his value.'

But, as Gary Inrig in his tremendous book *Quality Friendships* points out, 'Friendships are not simply found, they are built.' Take David and Jonathan as an outstanding example.

We read that David was being hunted by King Saul and was hiding in a forest. *'Then Jonathan,'* says the Scripture, *'Saul's son arose and went to David in the woods and strengthened his hand in God. And he said to him, "Do not fear, for the hand of Saul my father shall not find you. You shall be King over Israel, and I shall be next to you. Even my father Saul knows that."'*

It was the very last time we read of David and Jonathan being together. Soon Jonathan would die in battle and the two friends would be permanently separated.

What an unlikely pair they were. Contrast them. David treated as an outlaw and Jonathan the heir apparent to Israel's throne. Surely they were potential enemies, rivals, even, but God had brought them together.

Jonathan had everything to lose by his friendship with David, but Jonathan saw beyond his own circumstances and recognised David's great need and reached out to meet it.

Jonathan was a giver. His name means 'The Lord has given'.

What did Jonathan give? He gave encouragement which is the oxygen of the soul. Is there any lovelier expression in all of Scripture than the expression that Jonathan *'Strengthened his (David's) hand in God'*.

You would never think such a man would have needed such encouragement to depend on God. Was not David a man after God's own heart?

Was he not the author of the greatest psalms of praise ever written? Was he not a great musician, a military strategist and the hero of the valley of Elah?

Did not his smooth stone bring the giant of Philistia crashing down? Have not the women of Israel sung and danced to his praise?

Was not Christ to be named as David's greater son? What would a man like that need encouragement for? We all need encouragement.

And David was no exception. Do not let people's position ever blind you to their needs. David's life was now threatened and he was faced with the possibility of bitterness and discouragement.

Jonathan was sensitive to that. He did not minimise David's problem, he did not behave unrealistically but just got down to the woods where David was and encouraged him to be directly dependent on God.

The later psalms that David wrote proved just how effective Jonathan was.

Did Jonathan's background make him such an effective friend? Certainly not. His father was just a pathetic character whose army had fallen from 330,000 to 600 men. There were only two swords to be found in all Israel (1 Samuel 13 v 22).

His father was also someone who had disobeyed God.

Jonathan also came from a quarrelsome home (1 Samuel 14 vs 49-50) and yet he became the great encourager of one of the greatest men of God this world has ever known.

It proves that you can have a great ministry of friendship to others even though you have the most difficult of backgrounds and the most difficult of circumstances.

If you are a Christian you know the Father is your creator, the Son is your redeemer and the Holy Spirit is your enabler.

You have a far greater revelation of God's grace than Jonathan ever did and far more reason to trust God. So, reach out today and strengthen someone's hand in God.

Please. There can be no telling what the repercussions will be.

9

Keep Your First Love

You know how it is. The honeymoon couple arrive home and soon the man goes out to work. The young bride gives him a kiss through the open car window and waves goodbye from the gate.

A year later she waves goodbye from the front doorstep. Five years later she waves goodbye from the kitchen window. Ten years later she does not wave at all!

What has happened? She has left her first love.

There is a young fellow in love. He will do anything for his girlfriend.

There are boxes of chocolates, red roses, gifts of perfume, phone calls; he dances attention upon her.

Marriage eventually comes and five years later, even less, where are the chocolates, the red roses, the gifts of perfume? He never phones her from the office unless he wants something.

What has happened? He has left his first love.

I'm sure you have seen what I am writing about with your own eyes. But have you seen it happen in a local church?

Take Ephesus. Our Lord commended Ephesus. 'I know your work,' he said. They were serving him well, even to the cost of pain.

'I know your patience', he commends them, for not only did they serve him and serve him well but they did it all patiently.

'I know you can't bear evil men', says the Lord of the churches and praises them for rooting out men who said they were apostles but weren't.

'You bore for my name's sake', says the one whose eyes miss nothing. It surely was the most remarkable church.

Yet, the one whose eyes were as a flame of fire detected something, 'I have against you that you have left your first love', he said.

That is all. No other sentence. No other word. And yet how much he has said.

First love defies analysis. It is unselfish, ardent, humble. It is bright with promise and the master missed it in the church at Ephesus.

He missed their song at the unusual hour. The emotion and the enthusiasm was missing.

Judas Iscariot would have had no trouble with the church at Ephesus. Why did he criticise Mary at Bethany? Because her love went beyond the bounds of dull regularity. You couldn't measure Mary's love on scales. It was beyond calculation.

She poured out her alabaster box of fervour.

G. Campbell Morgan described the church at Ephesus as being 'faultily faultless, icily regular, splendidly null'.

And so the challenge to our hearts is very clear. Are we serving Christ out of first love motivation?

Even if I defend the truth without first love I'll do more harm than good. I could contend for the faith with a spirit which is in conflict with faith.

Activity for the King will not make up for neglect of the King.

The message of the Lord to the church at Ephesus was to *'Remember'* from where they were fallen and to *'Repent'* - to turn back and to do those works they once did out of first love.

Lift your mind, soul and heart to your lovely Lord, just now, Christian. As Peter said, 'Lord you know all things, you know that I love you'.

Tell your Lord that every day. Don't let anything cool or spoil your first love for the Lord Jesus.

10

Trial By Fire

He sat there, looking me straight in the eye and uttered words that have burned in my mind for days. He had just suffered two great losses in his life - one alone would have caused most people to buckle.

He told me he was faced with two conclusions, 'Either God is vindictive or else he is trying to say something to me.' He didn't believe the first and he was leaning hard on the second.

So was Peter when he wrote, *'The trial of your faith, being much more precious than of gold that perisheth, though it be tried with fire, might be found unto praise and honour and glory at the appearing of Jesus Christ'* (I Peter 1 v7).

I am convinced that the Lord - the greatest of all refiners - uses fiery trials to prepare Christians for greater and more useful service.

There are trials we bring upon ourselves and there are trials brought on by others, but although God permits them both there are trials sent to us by God himself.

Remember, the Lord's refining fire is proof there is something precious in us. Otherwise he would not spend so much time on us.

Have you ever heard of a refiner casting stones into a crucible? You must be capable of some higher service which can only be secured by being plunged into the refining fire.

The Lord permits the trial but he also superintends it, watching its progress and knowing when it should stop. Fire burns with intensity all impurity away from objects committed to it.

I have seen it so often in my life. Pride, selfishness, jealousy and envy, impatience and ungratefulness - they all appear like scum and the gracious refiner again and again turns the flame into our circumstances.

We are not the sport of blind fate nor change. There is no such a thing as luck or mere coincidence. The Lord uses trial to burn off the dross, the impurities or the chaff. It humbles us, proves us, enriches us.

Have you not heard Christians say, 'I've never known the presence of God to be so real. How do people cope who do not know the Lord?'

Look at the refining fires in the lives of those Bible characters who learned to wait for God: Joseph, Abraham, David, Ruth, Hannah, and many more.

Is the gold not well repaid for the fires when it sits on the Queen's head? Is the diamond not well repaid for the cutting when it glistens on Princess Diana's neck?

Will you not be all the more compensated for all your trials when you see how they have wrought out the eternal weight of glory? I tell you, you will be more than compensated.

Britain's great record-beating athlete Steve Cram ran in Budapest. He was leading the race at the half-way stage when his pacemaker dropped out and he had no first class challengers.

'It was very, very tough', he said. 'I'm not going to do anything like that again for a long time'.

Even world-class athletes need pressure to make them do better. *'Now they do it to obtain a corruptible crown; but we an incorruptible'* (I Corinthians 9 v 25).

Think of a shy little boy whose family were forced out of their home when he was seven. He had to work to help support them.

At nine his mother died. At 22 he lost his job as a shop clerk. He wanted to go to law college.

At 23 he asked the girl he loved to marry him and she said no. At 37 he was elected to the US Congress on his third try. Two years later he failed to be re-elected. He had a nervous breakdown.

At 41 his four-year-old son died. At 45 he ran for the Senate and lost. At 49 he lost in his second run for the Senate. At 51 he was defeated for nomination for Vice-President.

He was despised by multitudes, misunderstood, had periods of deep depression, was snubbed and at 56 was gunned down and died in a little room I have stood in. The blood-stained pillow still lies there, preserved as a memorial to the greatest US President who ever lived.

One night a friend of his was staying with him in the White House and happened to catch a glimpse of him through an open door kneeling before an open Bible. He heard him say, 'O thou great God who heard Solomon in the night when he prayed and cried for wisdom, hear me.

'I cannot lead these people. I cannot guide the affairs of this country without thy help. O Lord, hear me and save this nation'. The Union was preserved.

He learned to wait for God. His trials made him into a great man. So will yours if you are exercised by them, learn from them accept them as from a loving hand.

His name was of course Abraham Lincoln. What's yours?

Will they ever raise a statue to your memory? I'll tell you one thing" I never saw a statue raised to a critic in my life.

Don't just read and criticise history - make it. But you'll have to go through God's fires first. Be prepared.

11

Have A Talk With Yourself

'Were you talking to yourself, dad?', my children often ask me. I have to confess to them that I often have been. They look at me as if I were senile.

Well, I'm not senile and I find I have biblical authority for talking to myself. It is good therapy.

In Psalms 42 and 43 the depressed writer finds life hard going. Tears keep coming day and night.

He has been away up in the northern part of Israel and cannot get to Temple worship in Jerusalem. He is spiritually thirsty and and his enemies who worship gods they can see, mock him and think it is a huge joke that he worships an unseen God.

Unfortunately, the deeply discouraged and depressed psalmist had been indulging in a sin in which it is so easy to indulge; he had been complaining against God.

'Why have you forgotten me?', he asks God. 'Why have you cast me off?', he complains.

The fact is God never forgets his children. Never. 'Can a mother forget the child she bore?' asks God. The answer is that she may.

'Yet,' says God, 'I will never leave you nor forsake you.' It is a sin to complain against God.

Remember it is not a sin to weep like the Psalmist wept. Some Christians think it is our duty to go around with a permanent grin. Tears are part of a Christian's integrity.

Did not our lovely Lord weep twice, once at the grave of Lazarus and then over the spiritual condition of the city of Jerusalem?

When did you last see a Christian leader weep? It is almost a sign of weakness to weep today. It is almost as if folk are saying a weeping Christian is not full of the Spirit of God.

God knows if we were truly filled with the Spirit we would weep a lot more. No - a million times no - it is *not* a sign of weakness to weep. As we look around our world today, let us ask ourselves why we do not weep more for the incredible plight it is in and the spiritual darkness in which it is enveloped .

The psalmist fortunately turned away from confronting God to confronting himself. Instead of asking God why, he asked himself why. This is a much healthier thing to do. It is wrong to turn on God and say, 'Why have you forgotten me?' but it is not wrong to turn on yourself and say, 'Why are you so downcast? What is the cause of your depression?'.

I say to you, depressed one, take the initiative and talk to yourself. I often talk to myself when I get discouraged.

Why, this very day I felt discouraged and while I was writing this article a young man arrived at my door with a gift of all kinds of lovely fish for me and my family to eat. There was rainbow trout, cod fillets, prawns and more - and a big smile to go with it.

As he left he said to me, 'You have been feeding me

on God's Word when the whole world seemed to be on my shoulders and I have been refreshed. Now I am feeding you!'

When he had gone I talked to myself about forgetting what God was doing through his Word which it is my great privilege to preach weekly in the great city of Belfast.

May I reverently ask: 'Did not the Lord Jesus talk to himself?' He certainly did. *'Now is my soul troubled; and what shall I say? Father, save me from this hour: but for this purpose came I unto this hour'* (John 12 v 27). So, talk to yourself in the midst of your depression today. Stop searching for reasons and start resting on promises.

Say to yourself, 'Now if I was in hospital with a couple of broken legs and the doctor came and told me he stitched this to that and injected me with that for this, would that really fire my heart?'

It would be interesting but it would not fire you on much. yet, if the doctor said, 'Tomorrow you can to home and in two months you will walk again.' Would that encourage you? Of course it would.

Promises are much better than explanations. Trace your depression and you will soon find the thing that is discouraging you.

Take God's promises and bombard the source of your depression - a hurtful word, a mistake, a sin, unemployment or whatever - with the promises of God.

Go on, take a cue from the psalmist: *Why are you cast down, O my soul? And why are you disquieted within me? Hope in God: for I shall yet praise him who is the health of my countenance, and of my God'.*

I hope there will be thousands upon thousands of

my readers talking to themselves all over this country this week.

Let's make it 'Talk to yourself week'! Healthy countenances will result. Just ask the psalmist.

12

Do You Ever Doubt?

They come to me with sadness in their eyes. They are downcast and often depressed. They have waited for God, often, and even trusted his Son for salvation but they have begun to have doubts. Many of them wonder if they will go to hell for doubting.

Often I tell them the story of John the Baptist's doubts. He had waited for God to send the Messiah and his long wait was eventually rewarded with the appearance of the Lord Jesus by the Jordan river.

Gladly John pointed him out as the Lamb of God and the great sin bearer.

The ministry of the Christ began and John found himself in prison for his faithful stand against the sins of Herod.

It must have been very depressing in prison and slowly nagging doubts about the authenticity of the Messiah came into John's mind.

The fiery darts of the evil one became a flame. Matthew says, *'When John had heard in prison about the works of Christ he sent two of his disciples and said to him, "Are you the coming one or do we look for another?"'*

How would you have dealt with John's question? Did the Lord Jesus write John off for his doubts?

Certainly not.

'Go and tell John the things which you hear and see', said the Lord. *'The blind receive their sight and the lame walk: the lepers are cleansed and the deaf are made to hear; the dead are raised up and the poor have the Gospel preached to them and blessed is he who is not offended because of me.'*

This was a quotation from Isaiah prophesying what the Messiah would do when he came. Christ was reminding John that he had fulfilled those prophesies to the letter.

We never read that John ever doubted again. He had momentarily forgotten the promises of God in the depressing flood of personal circumstances. And don't millions of other believers?

At such a moment Satan throws the fiery dart of doubt. But just because the doubts arise it does not mean the the soul is lost. Mark the words of Christ following his reminder to John of fulfilled promises.

As John's disciples departed, *'Jesus began to say to the multitudes concerning John: "What did you go out into the wilderness to see? A reed shaken by the wind? ... There has risen no one greater than John the Baptist: but he who is least in the Kingdom of heaven is greater than he."'*

Christ certainly did not consider John's soul lost because John had doubted; rather Christ dispelled John's doubts.

Jesus *can* dispel your doubts and fears with the constant fulfilling of his promises.

No matter what Satan throws at you, the Lord can match it with a promise.

And the least in the Kingdom of heaven is greater than John: why? Maybe because they have not seen, like John and doubting Thomas did, but yet have believed.

George Matheson the great hymn writer and

preacher once had an eclipse of his faith and got very depressed. His elders fortunately dealt with him with understanding and gentleness and soon the flickering faith of the great man of God was burning brightly again.

For millions Matheson's great hymn has beautifully expressed God's way of dispelling all doubts. Meditate on its meaning today and you will be praying, 'Lord I believe' help my unbelief!'

> *O love, that wilt not let me go,*
> *I rest my weary soul in thee.*
> *I give thee back the life I owe,*
> *That in thine ocean depths its flow*
> *May richer, fuller be.*
>
> *Oh joy, that seekest me through pain,*
> *I cannot close my heart to thee;*
> *I trace the rainbow through the rain,*
> *And feel the promise is not vain*
> *That morn shall tearless be.*
>
> *O cross that liftest up my head,*
> *I dare not ask to fly from thee;*
> *I lay in dust life's glory dead*
> *And from the ground their blossoms red,*
> *Life that shall endless be.*

13

The Interrupted Prayer

A lady who returned from Africa recently dined out with some friends. She was so aghast at the wasted food at the end of the meal she automatically found herself collecting it up for further use.

After years of exposure to an environment filled with great poverty, the lady was suddenly aware of the incredible waste of food here in the West.

But is food all that we waste? What is waste anyway? It is the taking of the substance of life and expending it in such a way as to squander it without any abiding satisfaction or proper return.

The prodigal son *'wasted his substance with riotous living'*. Riotous means without saving.

He took his father's gifts, and spent them in the far country without making provision for leaner days and the ultimate needs of life.

Notice it was his father's gifts he wasted. His father had divided 'his living' among two sons. All the forces that were originally from God are being expended today in iniquity and wickedness.

The root idea of the word 'substance' is that of being, all the forces from God that make life. Back of the loaf, the flour; back of the flour, the mill; back of the mill, the miller; back of the miller, the farmer; back of the farmer, the seed; back of the seed, the sun; back of the sun, God.

All man's resources are divine gifts. God gave me energy to live. I cannot recall a single ounce of energy I have expended. What am I doing with it?

What about the mental powers the Lord gives to me? What about the powers of thought, observation, comparison, deduction? I am spending them. For what?

Or what about the moral powers to choose and to love good and to hate evil?

What of the spiritual forces that open up to me an awareness of eternity and give me a vision of things greater than earthly kings and cabbages?

The prodigal had got to the far country and the Saviour distinctly said that he had *'spent all'*.

The far country had no currency of its own, you know. *'No man gave to him'*, Scripture says. His friends had done a disappearing act when the prodigal had spent all.

I wonder whether you are in the far country.

As Vance Havner put it, 'The far country is not hard to find. You can enter it right where you are; you do not have to go to Las Vegas. You can even be a church member, teaching a Sunday school class, and live in it.

'There have been preachers who lived in the far country but preached in pulpits every Sunday. It is a state of mind, or the heart and of the affections. It is rebellion against the Word and will of God. It is measured in terms of distance between a man and the Lord.'

What was the prodigal son's greatest adventure? It was that he escaped from the operation of the strongest and most imperative law in the scheme of things. It is the law that binds us to our burdens and reconciles us to the necessity of carrying them.

Why does the parent robin go on feeding the cuckoo who has already shoved her offspring from their nest and now lie dead on the ground below?

Why does the parent bird protect the murderer of her offspring? Because by the time the parents discover the cuckoo's true character they have become attached to him!

They have cared for him so long they can't treat him harshly. They fall in love with the tyrant and cherish him!

It is a strange law in life that we get attached to and grow to love burdens we could shed right now. Thank God the prodigal son never got so accustomed to the far country that he couldn't break away from it.

At last he left the hog wash for the father's house. He might not have lived to go back. He might have gone back too late.

He might have gone back to find his father changed. He might have returned impenitent with no change of heart. He might have relapsed into prodigalism. None of these things happened.

Of course, when the waster returned his elder brother thought the feast was too good for him. He thought he had forfeited his rights; he thought his degradation would continue.

His prayer to his father was an interrupted one. I ask you, was there ever a prayer more gloriously interrupted?

He meant to say, 'I have sinned against heaven and before you and am no more worthy to be called your son; make me as one of your hired servants'. He never got that far because his father called, among other things, for a pair of sandals to be put on his feet.

A slave was never permitted to wear sandals. The sandals showed that his was to be the service of a son, not a slave.

So if you are a waster, Christian, repent and return to the Father and he will abundantly pardon you. If you are a waster, non-Christian, repent and come on home to the Father and he will do for you what no farmer could ever do.

What's that? He will restore to you the years that the locusts have eaten.

Remember you cannot save time, you can only spend it. Spend it for the Master and it will never be wasted. Not a moment of it.

14

Forgiveness Puts The Singing Back

Queen Victoria's grief was inconsolable after the death of her husband, Prince Albert. In the evenings she would weep as a lady-in-waiting read her passages from the Scriptures.

One of them even ventured to reason with Victoria; 'Your majesty, instead of feeling morbid, you should rejoice. One day in heaven you will meet the great people from the Bible - Moses, Jacob, Abraham, Solomon, David ...'

'No! No!' interjected Queen Victoria, 'I will not meet David!'

Poor David, even Queen Victoria didn't want to meet him. So it is with people when they fall into sin. There is very little mercy for them.

One such could just happen to be reading these lines. You are a believer and yet you have been tripped up by the subtlest of all enemies, Satan himself.

Few people have shown you any mercy or comfort since your sad error and sin. Has the Bible anything to say to you of comfort and help? It certainly has.

'Blessed is he whose transgression is forgiven, whose sin is covered. Blessed is the man to whom the Lord does not impute iniquity, and in whose spirit there is no guile' (Psalm 32 vs 1-2).

There are four words used here: transgression, sin, iniquity, guile. Transgression means rebellion. Sin means to miss the mark, iniquity means to be morally crooked and guile means cunning.

David knew all four of these things in his life but for about a year after his sin with Bathsheba and his murder of Uriah, Bathsheba's husband, he refused to confess his sins to God.

Instead of making things better it made them worse. His vitality was sapped. *'My vitality was turned into the drought of summer,'* he said, and he also knew the chastening hand of God upon him.

Does that describe you today? The way to help is to confess to the Lord that you have sinned.

Eventually David got to that point: *'I will confess my transgression to the Lord,'* he wrote. *'And you forgave the iniquity of my sin.'*

Yet let me try to emphasis a great truth here. Psychologists teach the vital importance of confession and the relief that comes to a distressed individual as a result.

But the forgiveness God gives is not just the relief of confession. It is far, far deeper than that.

Eighty per cent of all mental institutions are filled with people who have feelings of guilt, I'm told. How can we know we are truly forgiven?

Notice the word used by David. *'Blessed is he whose transgression is forgiven, whose sin is covered.'*

What does he mean? Football managers and politicians, even schoolteachers and doctors are often used as 'scapegoats'.

The term scapegoat has come into the English language meaning a person made responsible for the shortcomings of others.

It originally comes from the Hebrew system of sacrifice and forgiveness. A goat would be selected by the high priest who would lay his hands on its head, confess over it the sins, iniquities and transgressions of the people and thereby in a ceremonial fashion, put the weight of the sin on the goat.

The animal was then sent away into the wilderness. The children of Israel had a graphic reminder of how God puts our sins *far away* from him.

The wonderful truth is that since our Lord Jesus came and bore in his own body our sins on Calvary, as soon as we trust him as Saviour our sins are *out of sight*. They are covered.

David says even more. He says our sins will not be reckoned to us, or counted against us. God will not put them on our account.

Christ has accepted full responsibility for them. That does not set you free to do as you like but it sets you free to do as God likes.

Is it any wonder that David says, *'Be glad in the Lord and rejoice, you righteous: and shout for joy all you upright in heart!'*

Sin takes singing out of your heart but forgiveness puts it back in again. Sing, forgiven one, sing!

15

Christ's Heartbeat

You couldn't study Christ's letter to the Church at Laodicea without feeling the heartbeat of the Son of God.

Christ tells the Laodicean Church that he is the 'Amen'. That means he is the conclusion, the last word, the end to which nothing can be added.

He tells them he is *'Faithful and true witness'*. That means when he speaks there is no exaggeration and no minimising done.

He says he is *'the beginning of the creation of God'*. This means that when he speaks he comes as the one whose footprints can be traced throughout all creation.

In the beautiful and gorgeous robing of the autumn soon to blaze across the forests and countrysides of Europe, the very power of Christ is to be discovered. When Christ speaks to a church they had better listen.

First the Lord describes the general condition of the Church at Laodicea; *'You are neither hot nor cold'*, he says. They were not utterly indifferent. They were not fervently zealous. They were tepid; not frozen, not boiling. Tepid.

The Lord would rather they had been cold or boiling, but to be tepid was utterly repugnant to him. They had no enthusiasm, no urgency, no compassion.

They were evangelical but not evangelistic. The cross was not denied but it was not vital. Sin was admitted but there was no hatred.

What did the Laodicean Church think of itself? They said they were rich and had need of nothing.

Christ's view was that they were *'wretched'*. That means they were oppressed with a burden.

The burden was that they were very wealthy and imagined their wealth carried them. Instead it burdened them and degraded them.

This Church was not burdened with debt. It was burdened with wealth!

'You are miserable', said the Lord. This means the Lord pitied them.

'You are poor', he said. This means they possessed nothing worth having.

'You are blind', he adds. They could see nothing. They lacked vision and were confined within a narrow limit.

'You are naked', he tells them. That means they were stripped of the glory and beauty which ought to adorn a church of Jesus Christ.

Every word Christ spoke to this Church were words of pity. Yet what was his counsel to the conceited Christians of Laodicea? What advice did he give to the Church which was such an insipid lukewarm concoction that the Lord Jesus said he would spit it out of his mouth - put them away from the place of witness and testimony?

He told them there was an alternative. he told them he possessed all the Church lacked. He said *'Buy of me gold refined by fire'*.

You cannot buy spiritual power, you know, you can only have it by repentance and being yielded to the Spirit of God.

Money can buy medicine but not health; a house but not a home; companionship but not friends; entertainment but not happiness; food but not an appetite; a bed but not sleep; a crucifix but not a Saviour. Money has never yet made anyone rich.

'Buy my gold', says the Lord. *'I'll give you white raiment'* said the righteous one. *'I have eyesalve'*, says the great physician, *'I'll lengthen your vision, I'll make things clear'*.

'I care', he is saying, *'As many as I love I reprove and chasten'*. *'Be zealous and repent'*. *'I'll wait.'*

'Behold I stand at the door and knock, if any man hear my voice and open the door, I will come in to him and will sup with him, and he with me.' Are you that person.

16

You Are Invited To A Banquet

Do you like banquets? Good, because there is an invitation for you to go to the banquet of all banquets.

The host is no killjoy; when he hangs out his bunting no one will be disappointed with what goes on. Satisfaction is guaranteed.

There is no lovelier description in all of the Scriptures of the delights of the coming kingdom than when the Saviour described it as: *'They shall come from the east, and from the west, and from the north, and from the south, and shall sit down in the kingdom of God'* (Luke 13 v 29).

'To sit down' in Greek means to *'recline at the table'* which was, of course the Middle Eastern way of eating.

Can you imagine what a gathering of faith and experience that will be? People will be going to that banquet from every period of history; *'You shall see Abraham, Isaac and Jacob and all the prophets'* said Christ.

All present will talk of their experiences with God along life's journey. Never will there have been such a delightful swapping of stories that really matter.

A table in Scripture is often used as a metaphor. The table speaks of the infinite delights which Christ has obtained for his people.

It speaks of a whole eternity of heaven and the schemes God has designed to fill it.

Sadly, there is also a table of the lost. It is not without its pleasures but the tragic thing is that its joys become a snare, a trap and a stumbling block (see Romans 11 v 9).

One of the most vivid and tragic cases of someone who ended up eating at the table of the lost was King Saul. He began in a palace but ended up a disguised guest of a spirit medium with the witches of Endor. He did his best to enjoy himself for he knew the next day would bring tragedy.

Again and again God sought to draw Saul to himself but he refused. He lived for his own schemes and followed his own tastes and the wages of sin was death.

At which table do you feed? The table of the saved or the table of the lost? It is a vital question to ask.

'Blessed is he that shall eat bread in the kingdom of God,' said an unnamed listener to Christ. The statement brought a parable to the Saviour's lips.

He told of a man who prepared a lavish banquet. It was no mere meal but his invited guests intentionally missed it.

They would have attended but they had no wish to. They had other things to do.

They like multitudes in our world today enjoy the Creator's gifts but the Creator himself they regard as a bore. They reckon, without ever tasting what the Master of the house has to give that it would never please them. They will have their choice, for Christ said, *'They shall never taste of my supper'*.

One man in the parable had two good legs for he had to go and test his yoke of oxen; that was his excuse for not going to the banquet. Others whose legs were crippled got into the banquet and stayed.

Another had two good eyes because his excuse was that he had to go and see land which he had bought. Others who had no sight got into the banquet and stayed.

Another had attracted a woman's love, and he used his marriage to her as an excuse.

Others who were horribly maimed and no woman would ever dream of marrying got to the feast instead.

So it will be in the coming day: those who refuse the Gospel in life will find God has left them with their choice. Those who gladly receive it will go to enjoy pleasures at God's right hand for evermore.

The invitation to this banquet goes out to all men everywhere and it is a free invitation. Make no mistake, though, it is not cheap. Christ taught that if receiving it as a gift involved the loss of everything else, we would be foolish not to accept it.

It may cost you a lot in terms of career and friends and even family to accept Christ as your Saviour, but it is infinitely worth the loss of all things to win Christ.

I was preaching the Word of God every morning in a tent in the city of Anyany in South Korea. One morning after finishing my message a woman came running to me and threw her arms around me and hugged me.

I called my interpreter over to discover what she was saying to me. 'She is saying', said the interpreter, 'that yesterday morning she came to the service in the tent and discovered for the first time in her life that the Lord Jesus had died for her at Calvary'.

'She is saying that she could not sleep last night for the sheer thrill of knowing she would never have to face a God of judgment'.

I asked the lady her name and she told me it was Yang Soon Lee and she was 81 years old.

Could it be that an 81-year-old Korean woman who believed the Gospel of Christ the first time she heard it will get into the kingdom of God before some reader of this column? Why? Because that reader may have heard the Gospel of Christ and its lovely invitation hundreds of times and refused to accept Christ as their personal Saviour.

Let me tell you this: there certainly is a place for you at that coming banquet if you will repent of your sin and accept the Saviour. With all my heart I recommend you to receive the host's invitation. *Selah.*

17

Pie In The Sky?

Many people think the Christian faith is all promises - pie in the sky when you die. They foolishly despise a faith so full of promises.

It is a good question though - why does God deal in promises? Why does he make so many? Because of the way we are made.

A very essential part of our human personality is that we have desires. The pen I am writing with has no desires. It stays where I put it, but we are made with desires.

We are not content to sit around; we are motivated to live and move by desires. That is how God made us.

God, because he gave us desires, gave us promises to touch those desires. The Apostle Peter says, God has given us *'exceeding great and precious promises'* (2 Peter 1 v 4) to get us on the move.

Peter says it was the Lord's glory and goodness that flamed his desires. He says he was drawn by the Lord's *'glory and virtue'* (2 Peter 1 v 3) and, of course, he was ready and willing to lay down his nets and follow such a good and glorious master.

I don't know why you came to Christ, but to come to him for salvation because you are lonely or want to escape God's judgment, and not to be interested in the Lord or in making progress in the Christian life would be a disaster.

It is vital that our desires are focussed on him and this will make us want to be like him.

Peter says we are to escape *'the corruption that is in the world through lust'*. This is implying that the world is very interested in our desires. Nothing could be more accurate.

The world plays on our desires, no matter what age we are and is committed, through our desires, to wage a life and death struggle with our soul. It is vital where we focus our desires.

Peter teaches that all the necessary things are given to Christians to make progress in the Christian life - *'As his divine power has given us all things that pertain to life and godliness.'*

Does that mean we are to do nothing? If God has promised that all the necessary things are given, does that mean we cruise on into Christ's eternal kingdom.

Let me answer that question by asking you another question. When you were born did you quote Shakespeare to your mother? No? But you had the potential to, didn't you?

You certainly had, and after hard work at school you could quote the odd line of *Hamlet* or *Romeo and Juliet* to your mother over a cup of coffee any morning she would choose to ask you.

Now, God has given you the potential you need for your Christian life but you must get out there and work at adding things to your faith. They won't come automatically.

'Add to your faith, virtue', says Peter. How could you do that? By being good at everything you do. At behaving, for example. How could you be good at

behaving if you didn't get out there and behave?

'*Add to your faith, knowledge*'. How could you gain knowledge if you didn't learn it through experience and the reading and studying of the Scriptures? That will take a lot of effort.

'*Add to your faith, self control*'. How could you add self control to your faith if you sat alone in your chair and never got involved with people?

We are also to add '*endurance*', the ability to stick with something and '*Godliness*', the development of our walk with God; '*brotherly kindness*', which is love for fellow Christians and '*agape love*' which is love for even the unlovable.

If you and I keep busy adding these things to our faith we will not come a cropper. We will not get caught up with false doctrine and be diverted from following our Lord closely.

Add these things to your faith and '*an entrance will be supplied to you abundantly into the everlasting kingdom of our Lord and Saviour Jesus Christ*'.

Notice it does not say an '*entry*'; every Christian will be granted an entry, but every Christian will not be granted a rich entrance.

A rich entrance is not just to get through the door of heaven - but is an ability to enter into the great activities God will lay on to the maximum.

So, there is no time to waste for any of us. Let's up and at it. Let God's promise flame your desire to follow him and obey him today.

18

A Cool Hand On A Hot Head

Just as God's mercies are new every morning, so are Satan's schemes. One of those schemes nearly ditched David but was averted by one of the most beautiful women in all of Scripture. Let's learn some lessons from the story.

David and his men on the run from King Saul were looking for 'a tip' for protecting a sheep baron's flock during sheep shearing time. The sheep baron, a man called Nabal, used very dismissive language of David. He accused him of insurrection and idleness. It was a very cruel construction on David's lifestyle.

Nabal was a fool and had no idea of the consequences of what he had said. He forgot all about it as soon as the words were spoken and we find them in his house, holding a feast like the feast of a king and soon, thoroughly drunk.

He was a rude, uncourteous slob. Totally ignorant of the causes which forced David out of Saul's house he raised David's temper as few men had ever done.

For months, self control had marked the man after God's own heart. Careful to constantly seek God's will, time and again, David had shown commendable self-restraint. Yet, David now rose with passion to Nabal's insult.

He got 400 of his men together and all of them, armed to the teeth, set out to kill the nasty sheep baron and every male servant in his entourage.

It is very easy for yesterday's victories to suddenly become today's temptations. Is it not true that the sin we shunned yesterday, we embrace today? Let's learn that you cannot live today on yesterday's obedience.

Blind anger was now leading David to the brink of crime and, of course, all the while feeling perfectly justified. He was about to shed blood causelessly and avenge himself, instead of leaving it to the Lord to deal with his enemies.

From this shame, sorrow and disgrace David was saved by the beautiful Abigail. No wonder her name meant 'whose father is joy'.

The Bible describes her as having 'a beautiful countenance and good understanding'. What a rare combination it is when beauty and brains combine. The two things do not always go together. there are many beautiful women who are desperately lacking in good understanding.

Good understanding is, in Scripture, more moral than it is intellectual and it puts 'a glow of beauty over the plainest features'.

In other words, as far as God is concerned, a woman can be beautiful without being good looking.

Isn't it remarkable, though, how many Abigails in this world get tied up with Nabals? I don't want to be too hard on Abigail because she may have been forced into marriage with Nabal by Eastern family tradition but let me put out a warning to any Christian woman contemplating marriage.

Do not let the advice of friends, the pressure of circumstances or the deceit of flattery push you into marriage with someone whom you don't love and who doesn't love you or your Lord. Such a situation would be a heartache that even time couldn't cure.

Do you know that famous Victorian painting called 'A Marriage of Convenience'? It shows an opulent home, a well-spread table, a butler in attendance but the wife of the home at one end of the table and the husband at the other.

A marriage of convenience is a disaster. If you marry for a lovely home or a good position you profane God's idea of marriage.

Yet Abigail, despite her narrow circumstance, immediately grasped the situation and dispatched 200 loaves of bread, 2 skins of wine, 5 dressed sheep, about 37 litres of roasted corn, 100 cakes of raisins, 200 cakes of pressed figs on the back of some donkeys and rode out to meet David and his men.

David was not waiting for God but by the time he and his men came down by 'the covert of the hill' here was this beautiful woman on her knees pleading with David to wait for God.

She admitted her husband's wrong, she depreciated her generous gift of food as only fit for David's servants, and gently hinted at a past act of faith by David, told him he would be better letting God take vengeance on his enemies and then he would experience God's power slinging his enemies out as a stone from a sling.

Abigail brought David back to his better self. He listened to her and took his men home to wait for God. He didn't have to wait long. Nabal died within days. Is it any wonder David married Abigail?

So, Abigails of the church, get out there and plead

with the present day Davids to 'wise up' and to wait for God. Will they listen to you? They just might. Call them from selfish passion and anger to a better way. Draw them to God's will and they will have reason for endless gratitude.

Yesterday's victories of the men after God's own heart do not have to become today's defeats. Abigails of the world, unite. I've got one in my house, thank God. Have you? Cherish her.

19

A Lick Of Paint

A lady stopped me in the city the other day. 'Derick,' she said earnestly, 'Do you think a Christian should wear make-up?' Such questions are not often asked me on a city street but this lady had just recently become a Christian and obviously had reason to ask.

'Well,' I said, 'There was once a very famous evangelist here in Ulster called W. P. Nicholson. One evening he asked all the ladies in his congregation who did not wear make-up to put their hands up. Many complied. With a glint in his eye the famous preacher then leaned over the pulpit and said, "Ah, Ladies, it is a poor old barn door that doesn't improve with a lick of paint!"'

There is another view, I pointed out to the lady on the street, which many believe. It is put like this:

'Dare to be a Daniel
Dare to stand alone
Dare to pass a Chemist's shop
And call your face your own!'

Scripture states of women's dress: *'Whose adorning let it not be that outward adorning of plaiting the hair and weaving of gold or of putting on of apparel but let it be the hidden man of the heart in that which is not corruptible, even the ornament of a meek and quiet spirit which is in the sight of God of great price'* (I Peter 3 vs 3-4).

Obviously the verse is not saying, 'Don't were jewellry' (see Proverbs 25 v 12), for if you take the verse to mean that then by the same interpretation you must take the verse to mean that you should wear no apparel either and that would never do!

The verse is saying that true beauty is not in wonderfully arranged hair or jewellry or clothes, it is character that really matters.

Cheer up, ladies, for this verse is saying that you don't have to be good-looking to be beautiful! Beauty in the eyes of God is much deeper and lasts longer than a *Vogue* cover and yet in no way is Scripture teaching that a Christian woman is to go around like an unmade bed all day!

Modesty is vital and an overdressed woman is always despised even by non-Christians.

I often wonder about the purpose of that unopened cruet of ointment in the possession of Mary of Bethany. How did she come by it? It was maybe the bequest of a loving parent; maybe it was kept for her own wedding day: maybe she had bought it specifically to pour it out upon the Saviour's feet.

In any case it was her own. it did not belong to her brother or sister or to her household but to herself to be used as she wished and she devoted it to the honour of her Lord Jesus and had kept it against the day of his burial.

Was there ever such an amazing gathering of people as the day Mary poured out the ointment on Christ? Lazarus is there called from the corruption of the grave. his friends are there who recently wept at his grave and now are gathered to a feast to rejoice in his life.

Christ is there - the Prince of Life who is about to die! Judas is there grudging sorely at the waste of the costly ointment and inspired by the Prince of Darkness. But it is Mary who fills the story.

Mary was prepared for the work she was about to do. God the Father will have tribute paid to the honour of his Son before his death and he will have a fit servant to do it. Mary is that servant.

Mary speaks little. Of the seven sayings of Mary and Martha recorded, only one is Mary's. In Martha's house Mary listens and is silent. At her brother's grave she weeps and is silent. As she pours out the ointment of spikenard and anoints the feet of Jesus and wipes his feet with her hair she says nothing.

It was not that Mary did not think much, it was that here was a deep drinking in of the mind of Christ. She had waited at his feet. listening to his word. She knows that Christ is about to die. All the disciples have heard it often but in no-one except in Mary does it take the form of practical forethought and preparation.

The words of the Lord concerning his death have entered deep into Mary's heart and she will honour him in this death. Mary knows that her Lord will be betrayed into the hands of sinners and put to death so she pours the ointment over him as freely as Samuel shed the oil on the head of David.

Mary did what she could. It did not seem much but the smell of the ointment that filled the house at Bethany still fills the house of God, in one sense, even today.

Judas thought it a waste but here is a woman who in love expends in one hour nearly three times as much as the traitor is to gain by selling his soul to Satan and his Lord to the chief priests.

There were two prices set on the Saviour: the noble and the base. One penny was accepted as ample wages for a whole day's work. Three hundred of those pence would have hired 300 labourers for a day: but Mary pours it out on Christ.

Giving to the poor is a duty that may be done at any time but that which can be done at any time has to give way to that which has to be done now.

Mary acts and Mary chose that good part which shall not be taken away from her. Let us do a work for the Master in our day in his name and by his strength and for his glory. It will last much longer than a bottle of *Chanel* any day.

God will prepare you through faith for that work and give you the grace to carry it through. Trust him for the work in his own time. Wait for him, like Mary and your opportunity will come.

May your local church, your local community, your home and your heart be filled with the odour of your spikenard when the seal is broken.

Thousands may yet live to thank God for your ministry.

20

Buy Some Friends

'Is it fair?' people say. 'Is the teaching balanced?', they wonder. 'Is there something wrong with the whole idea?', they ponder. 'What's up?'

The problem has to do with the prodigal son repenting. People say the parable suggests it does not make any difference eternally whether you waste your life as a believer or whether you are faithful as long as you are repentant.

The answer to these probing questions about the parable of the prodigal son is that if we sinfully waste our lives and them come back to God in true repentance and faith, the fact that we have wasted our lives will make no difference at all to the pardon we shall receive or to our acceptance with the Father.

But, Jesus followed the parable of the prodigal son with another parable which puts the other side of the story.

In the following parable he taught that if you and I waste our lives it will, in another sense, make an eternal difference. Let me remind you of the mind bending parable.

Jesus told of a manager of a household who got

himself fired. When his boss called him in to deliver the bad news the manager realised he would need to act quickly because he had no means of supporting himself. He briefly considered getting a job digging ditches but decided against it and he dismissed begging because, although it wasn't work, it was too humbling.

Then he had a great idea. He reckoned that as he couldn't beg and wouldn't work, his only means of support was charity. But he had no means of knowing who would be charitable to him, so he decided to put some people in a position so they would feel obliged to be charitable.

There was one man who owed his boss more than 800 gallons of olive oil. He called the man and said, 'Take your bill and make it 400'. Then warming to his task he sent for another debtor who owed his boss a lot of wheat.

'How much do you owe?', he asked him. 'One thousand bushels of wheat', he said. 'Take your bill and make it 800', said the shrewd manager.

Both the oilman and the wheatman did not need telling twice. Off they went with the altered bills, rejoicing in their good fortune.

Shortly afterwards the boss found out what his manager had done and surprisingly the master commended the dishonest manager because he had acted shrewdly.

Nowhere in this parable are we asked to copy the steward's methods but certainly the Saviour is teaching us to copy his foresight.

Realising he would have to leave his job and not be able to control his master's goods much longer, he used his temporary stewardship of those goods to make friends for himself so that when he had to leave his job they would receive him into their home.

What are the practical lessons of this parable for Christians in these last few years of the 20th century? Well, first off, it is saying that nothing we have in this life belongs to us.

We brought nothing into this world and we shall take nothing out of it (1 Timothy 6 v 7). We are simply stewards. Even your time is only loaned to you; God could call it in at any moment.

Jesus himself, it has been said, spoke more about money than he did about any other subject. Your money is also only loaned to you and all or any of your possessions.

The prodigal son used his money to gain friends but how long did his friends last? As long as his money lasted.

You see the only measure of true worth and the final test of all values is permanence.

'What I spent I had, what I kept, I lost: what I gave, I have'.

'I tell you', said the Master, *'use worldly possessions and money to gain friends for yourself so that when your worldly wealth is gone you will be welcomed into eternal dwellings!'*

At the very heart of this great parable, heaven suddenly flashes into it. What will heaven be like? The plain teaching of this passage is that all will be equally welcome in heaven and all will be equally loved, but not all will have equally as many friends.

Do you not think if you give your money to, say, a project to win young folk in the Philippines for the Lord Jesus and a whole lot of them are subsequently won for Christ they will not show you an eternal gratitude which they will not show towards me if I merely spent all my money on my own enjoyment?

The searching question is that if we have not been faithful with earthly wealth, how can we be trusted with true wealth? True wealth is the eternal inheritance covenanted to us by Christ (Galatians 3: 15 v29).

Owning it is one thing but being put into the practical administration of it is another. If you, in your work for an earthly boss, have not been faithful in what belongs to another who will put you into active administration of your own things in an age to come?

Please, Christian, think long on that little phrase. *'Who shall give you that which is your own'* (Luke 16 v 12).

You cannot serve God *and* Mammon (earthly wealth or possessions) but you can serve God *with* Mammon to make yourself friends forever. If you use Mammon as an end in itself you are despising God and giving his second place.

So, I have a question for you. Do you really suppose, Christian, that a life spent despising God will make no difference when it comes to eternity? The lesson and challenge is loud and clear: let's go and make ourselves some friends for eternity, how about starting now?

21

The Devil Has No Truce

I have been thinking recently of a little poem which goes something like this:

Men don't believe in a Devil now,
As their fathers used to do;
They reject one creed because it's old
For another because it's new.

Who dogs the steps of the toiling saint?
Who spreads the net for his feet?
Who sows the tares in the world's broad field?
Where the Saviour sows his wheat?

They may say the Devil has never lived,
They may say the Devil is gone,
But simple people would like to know,
Who carries the business on?

Doggerel, maybe, but very true,
Right? Profound in fact.

Just try and resist the Devil for a little while and see if he is alive or not. you will find, as all believers have found, that the Devil never has a truce.

He never gives up. He relentlessly pursues the

Christian, sometimes subtly, sometimes blatantly, now lying back then opening up with a blitz.

He is, as Latimer put it in a sermon at St. Paul's Cathedral on 18th June 1548, 'The most diligent prelate and preacher in all England. He is never out of his diocese. He is never from his cure.

'Call for him when you will, he is ever at home. He is ever at his plough. No lording or loitering can hinder him.

'He is ever applying his business. You shall never find him idle, I warrant you.

'O that our prelates would be as diligent to sow the corn of good doctrine as Satan is to sow cockle and darnel. There was never such a preacher in England as he is.'

Preaching with my good friend, the late Dr. Alan Redpath once in the Republic of Ireland, I was brought up with a start when I heard him say there was no sin which he was not capable of committing two minutes after the service was over.

When I thought about it I was made aware of that chilling little verse in 1 Peter chapter 2 which says that fleshly lusts *War against the soul.*

War is war whether it is waged in an airliner with raw terror at Larnica airport or whether it is waged in a submarine 10.000 leagues under the sea.

The aim is to crush that which stands in the way of the will of the aggressor. Satan wages war and make no mistake about it, he is a dirty fighter.

How can he be defeated in the life of the Christian?

The Bible teaches that battles are always won before the armies take to the field. David dispatched Goliath in a few minutes but he had beaten him long before when he had proved God as he faced the lion and the bear.

The Lord Jesus won over Satan in the wilderness and Gethsemane before he faced him at Calvary.

Gideon pulled down Baal's altar in his dad's backyard before he ever defeated the Midianites who were before him as the sand on the seashore.

In any victory for God there is no skipping preparation. It does not matter who you are, there is no dodging it. If you meet the enemy without having first met God you can be certain what the outcome will be: in fact the outcome has already been decided. You will lose.

For the Christian the solution to preparation for Satan's attacks is found in submitting to God. It means putting ourselves under his control, under his authority.

Day by day we are called upon to walk in the Spirit. Of course the more you do that the more you will be open to the fierce attack of the evil one.

Is submitting to the authority of God enough? No, many a Christian has submitted but been constantly defeated. The Scripture teaches that we are to do two things: *'Submit yourselves therefore to God. Resist the Devil and he will flee from you'* (James 4 v 7).

After submitting we are to resist. In the physical and in the mental areas of our lives we must resist for all we are worth. We can only resist by keeping near to God and we cannot do that except through the Lord Jesus.

If you try to keep near to God without the Lord Jesus then you are only in the presence of a mysterious abstraction, but God has revealed himself in his precious Son and knowing him is knowing God. That means study of God's Word and prayer and work according to his will.

But there you have it. Submit and resist. Let those

two words into your very bloodstream.

Repeat them as you pass though the day. Repeat them as you pass into sleep. There is victory over Satan like you have never known it.

Submit and resist. Submit and resist. Submit and resist. Got it?

22

Silent Planet

There are millions of people in this world who suffer from a dumbness that is much more than physical dumbness. They are spiritually dumb.

Originally made to hold conversation with God, they never speak to him. They even say there is no Creator. If, after all, there is, they are not interested in talking to him for they say they don't know how to.

What's up? Why is it that when it is God's desire that men and women should articulate creation's response to the Creator, like a child talks to its father, millions of people don't? There must be an enemy at work, somewhere.

Someone must be crippling man's ability to speak with God and locking up man's spirit within himself. As far as God is concerned, the Enemy is turning this earth into what often appears to be a silent planet.

It was a great thing the Lord Jesus did the day he cast the demon responsible for a man's dumbness out of that man (see Luke 11 vs 14-26). But it was a far greater thing he did when he came and made it possible for people everywhere to be set free to talk to God.

Jesus taught in the parable immediately following

the miracle of the loosening of the dumb man's tongue that: *'When a strong man, fully armed, guards his own palace, his goods are in peace'*. That is a perfect description of the world in general.

Look at it! Look at the prayerless, spiritually dumb generation around you. They ask God for nothing. They do not even ask for deliverance.

Prayerless tongues by the million have been chained by the tyrant Satan who spares no energy in keeping them quiet with all kinds of devices.

And they are at peace under this strong one's guard, and even contented. The plain fact is, though, their peace is the peace of a prison.

Now, did the lovely Lord Jesus let the whole world lie in the lap of the wicked one? Certainly not.

He did not wait for the prisoners to invite him into their prison before he intervened. He took the initiative.

Strong and fully armed as the enemy was, Christ invaded this world by means of becoming a little baby. What a story!

Think of it! The Almighty appeared on earth as a helpless human baby unable to do more than lie and stare and wriggle and make noises, needing to be fed and taught to talk like any other child.

The more you think about it, the more staggering it gets. Our God contracted to a span, incomprehensibly made man.

When he grew up and went out into his public ministry the prisoners of Satan knew very well that here was something different. They began to listen and suddenly their eyes were opened to see they were in a prison.

Here was an authority, a compassion, a love, a power, a lifting of vision way out into eternity beyond denominations and factions and laws and petty squabbling and even the drudgery of every day life.

Here was life, but life that was more abundant. Here was purpose. Here was one who was encouraging people to break their silence and willing to set them free and able to get them talking to their Father.

'But,' said the Saviour, *'When a stronger man comes upon him* (ie a strong man) *and overcomes him, and takes from him all his armour in which he trusted and divides his spoils'.* That is what happened at the cross, for by Christ's death he invaded the very deepest of the Enemy's dungeons and broke his last stronghold.

Multitudes have been set free (Colossians 2 v 13-18: Hebrews 2 vs 14-15). Those who were once Satan's spoils have now become God's gifts to the Church (Ephesians 4 vs 7-13).

This is now by no means a silent planet. All over the world people have trusted Christ as Saviour and are talking to God! Dumbness has been replaced by praise.

If you are one of those who has been set free, then avail yourself of your privilege. Would there be anything sadder than someone who is dumb being healed and given the power of speech and not using it?

A little assembly of Christians met not all that long ago in the heart of the Ulster countryside. As they waited before the Lord at a time of 'open worship' at a breaking of bread service, no one spoke. The silence was deafening.

Suddenly a man over 80 years got up and gave out a hymn. Looking at those Christians straight in the eye he said with vigour: 'At least we can praise him!'

Indeed we can. That old man was my uncle. I rise up

and call him blessed for he said in that little sentence all I have been trying to say since the beginning of this article. *Selah*.

23

Please Make My Brown Eyes Blue

Amy was no mean young lady. She lived at Millisle in Co. Down and one night she got down on her knees to pray. 'Lord', she demanded, 'Please change the colour of my eyes. make them blue, like my mother's'.

The next morning the three year old Amy's eyes were as brown as ever. 'Lord', she prayed, 'I'll give you one more chance. Blue please, not brown'.

The next morning she leaped onto a chair, gazed in the mirror and she was almost convinced that her eyes were browner than they had ever been before.

'I'll never pray again', Amy told her mother, 'God didn't answer me'. 'He did', said her mother, 'He said "No" and isn't "No" an answer?'

Years later the girl from Millisle found herself passing through a place called Dohnavur in South India. She described it as 'A bare sunburnt spot out on the planes under the mountains to the west, a huddle of huts and small houses with an old ramshackle bungalow built of bricks and visibly falling to pieces.'

Early on the morning of march 6th 1901 Amy Carmichael was having early morning tea on the verandah when suddenly a little girl was brought to her. She was a very small and desolate mite with tumbled hair and troubled eyes. She ran straight to Amy climbed on her lap and said, 'My name is Pearl-eyes and I want to stay here always. I have come to stay.'

It transpired that Pearl-eyes' mother had been persuaded to devote her child to the gods. Once she managed to slip out and return to her mother but the temple women traced her, and her mother, threatened with the wrath of the gods, tore the child's arms from around her neck and gave her back to them. They branded her child's hands with hot irons. They said she had run away from a sacred calling. The 'sacred calling' was, of course, nothing less than child prostitution of unspeakable and obscene ferocity.

The British who ruled India turned a blind eye to the problem and so did the British missionaries who did not want to disturb their comfortable position with the Raj culture. The brown eyes from Millisle saw the unspeakable victim of it all standing before her and those brown eyes from Ulster refused to turn away.

The temple women came to the bungalow with a crowd. Pearl-eyes would not go with them and Amy would not force her. The crowd stoned the bungalow but Amy nor the child gave in. Pearl-eyes stayed and from her Amy learned at first hand of the secret traffic in the souls and bodies of little children. Amy described the things she learned as things that 'Darkened the sunlight'.

An overwhelming desire to save such children became a fire in Amy's bones. She went into the deep and foul abyss opening her eyes and starting to track down the helpless victims of such a hellish system, glorified by the sanctions of religion.

Few Ulsterwomen ever sacrificed more than Amy Carmichael as she settled at Dohnavur and year after year looked after those children under her care. The little sari-clad, dark haired dynamo carried a team around her called the Dohnavur Fellowship and had tasteful and purpose built buildings erected for her community of children in need. It became a haven for hundreds of them.

The children loved Amy but believe it or not there arose a fairly strong 'Get-Amy-Carmichael-Out-Of-India' among the Christian community in India. She was a thorn in their sides. Someone even said that her efforts to save 'Temple children' was nothing more than a stunt, meant to draw attention to herself. 'The temple system was centuries old, what did she think she could do about it? Preposterous allegations found ready acceptance. She was a dictator, her Indian girls worshipped her.'

But Amy went on. Her work prospered and the Lord was honoured. Though she died in 1951 the work she founded continues. Possibly millions of people have read her books.

It was Martha who scolded the Lord when he asked for the grave of Lazarus to be opened. 'There is a stench, he's been buried four days', complained Martha. But Christ wanted to prove to Martha and all the crowd who complained that he had been careless not to arrive before Lazarus had died that he did not just have power over death. He had power over decomposition! 'Lazarus come forth', he cried. If he had not said Lazarus, the whole graveyard would have come forth!

Don't get angry at God for not doing what you particularly want him to do. He knows what He is doing. One day a visitor to Dohnavur asked an Indian child as to why they all loved Amy Carmichael so much: 'That's easy', she replied, 'She's got the same colour of eyes as we have'.

24

Sowing Is Painful

Harvest is a lovely time of year. The crisp air, the falling leaves, the ploughed fields - it is a 'drawing-in' time. I love it.

Could I, just for a moment or two, contrast this delightful season with a less attractive time? I find some useful lessons for Christian service in the contrast.

I want to think about the differences between seedtime and harvest. *'Behold,'* said our Saviour, *'a sower went forth to sow'*. Sowing is a work of faith. It is a planting time.

You can see how many seeds are in an apple but you cannot see how many apples there are in a seed. Faith is very important at sowing time.

'He who observes the clouds will not sow' says the Scripture. It apples to all forms of Christian sowing too.

Travelling across the country I have noticed a strange phenomenon. When arriving in some city or town prior to commencing services I am often told that unfortunately it is a bad week for services.

Monday night there is a huge football match in town, Tuesday night there is a heavy metal rock concert, Wednesday night there is the final episode of a popular TV classic, Thursday is a general holiday in town, Friday the singing star Mr. X is at the town hall, and on Saturday, well, you know Saturday nights!

If I were to sit down with these people and discuss the matter, the first thing I would ask is, 'When is there ever a good week for Christian services and Bible teaching meetings?'

Would I wait, in this city of trouble, for an evening in which there were no bombs going off to teach my weekly Bible class? Would I wait until there was peace in Ulster before I would sow?

It seems to me they all start from the wrong point. The Word of God is always suitable and adequate for the needs of human hearts in any week.

We do not need to check the local paper or the *TV Times* to find out if it is suitable to preach God's Word. Others should be worried that there are Bible preaching meetings in town; not us! We should be a threat to *them*; not their attractions a threat to *us*.

'It's too cold,' says the fearful ploughman and does not plough and later begs. 'It's too difficult,' says the local church and never reaches out to the lost and no one is won for Christ.

'It's too late,' thinks the hardened sinner and perishes.

'It's not necessary now, it can wait until tomorrow,' they say and tomorrow never comes and 'it' waits forever.

The shortest way to ineffectiveness is to concern yourself with 'what ifs?' instead of the 'why nots'. If you let fear grip you, before you know where you are you will be strangled with the 'paralysis of analysis'.

Sowing for Christ is a lonely work. At harvest-time there is company and gaiety but as a rule the sower works alone. Sowing is a cheerless work.

The blue skies and warm sun of harvest-time are a contrast to the sombre, stern and cheerless days of seed-time.

Sowing is also a painful work, for sowing is imparting, flinging away, giving. Harvesting is gathering, getting, receiving. It is increase, enrichment.

Sowing brings disappointments, for out of a thousand seeds nature brings 'But one to bear'. Are you feeling brokenhearted today by the seeming failure of Christian work?

Remember that the Lord Jesus knew all about the cheerless, lonely, painful work of sowing. Yet he never murmured or complained.

Remember that the redeeming line in his parable is the little phrase, *'But some fell on good ground'.*

'He that goeth forth and weeping, bearing precious seed, shall doubtless come again with rejoicing bringing his sheaves with him.'

Lock him in a prison cell and you have a John Bunyan. Bury him in the snows of Valley Forge and you have a George Washington.

Deafen him and you have a Beethoven. Paralyse her and you have a Joni Eareckson Tada.

Call him a slow learner and uneducable and you have an Albert Einstein. Plant him in China with Gospel seed in his hand, heart-broken because his fiancee thousands of miles away in England won't marry him and have him criticised by other Christian missionaries because of his methods of trying to win the Chinese. Then you will have the life of Hudson Taylor and today you have 30 million Chinese Christians.

Are you a sower? Sow on.

25

Come On Out Of Prison

I love the story of Dick Saunders when he went into a prison to preach the Gospel to the inmates. Forgetting the setting Dick opened the Scriptures and spoke on the test from Hebrews, 'How shall we escape?'. He tells the story with a smile to this day. The message was, no doubt, well received!!

We think of the prisons of Britain at this time with all their overcrowding. We think of Broadmoor and Strangeways and those prisons of the past in other countries, like Alcatraz and Auschwitz. What an existence prison must be!

Yet there is a worse existence. If there is anything that will cripple your life it is the prison of an unforgiving spirit. There are a lot of people in such a self inflicted prison.

Jesus told us the parable about the man who was held in the prison of the unforgiving spirit. The setting of the parable is very clear. it all grew out of an argument about who should be the greatest in the kingdom (Matthew 18).

The Lord soon cured the disciples' mistake by pointing out that if he sent a mere child as his representative on some errand or other, how people received the child would be just as vital as to how they received an apostle.

Notice the emphasis is on the word 'receive'; *'Whoever receives one little child like this in my name receives me!'* The importance did not reside in the child or in the apostle but in the Christ they represented. It was a clear lesson in humility.

There followed the same very clear teaching on how we ought to treat someone who has offended us. We should go to the person who has offended us, privately. If that doesn't bring repentance we should take one or two believers along to pray and counsel with them. If that fails we should then take the issue to the church.

Peter, as he listened, had a problem. He wanted to know how often we should forgive someone. Seven times? Jesus said 490! I love Warren Wersbe's comment when he said; 'By the time you have forgiven somebody that many times, you are in the habit of forgiving and will not need to obey rules or set limits!

Christ then told of the king who audited his books and found that one of his servants owed him a million pounds. When the servant pleaded for time to pay, the king, out of the sheer compassion of his heart, forgave him and set him free.

On his way out the servant met a man who owed him £15. The man pleaded to be given time to pay but the servant had him arrested and put into prison.

When the king heard of it he had the servant delivered to jailers who tortured him until he paid what he owed. *'So'*, said the Saviour, *'my heavenly Father also will do to you if each one of you, from his heart, does not forgive his brother, his trespass'*.

Now the parable is not talking about salvation. But the parable is saying that if we are unable to pray

'*Forgive us our debts as we forgive our debtors*' then we, in practice, hound those who offend us, we might as well pray 'O God, I have sinned against you many times. I have forgotten your goodness and neglected your service.

'I have broken your laws. I have committed many secret sins. Deal with me as I deal with my brother. he hasn't offended or been ungrateful one tenth as much as I have been to you but I can't overlook his offence or ingratitude.

'I hold his behaviour against me in my heart, every inch of it. Deal with me as I deal with him.'

If we have an unforgiving spirit then we are, in effect, praying like this. So, let's repent and show forgiveness. An unforgiving spirit is a useless cause.

Forgive those who have wronged you and you will experience a joy and freedom and a lightness of spirit that only comes when you forgive as God has forgiven you.

He is not teaching that you do not seek to bring the one who has offended you to repentance but he is certainly teaching that whatever he does you must forgive him. So, come on out of prison Now.

26

The Heart-Stealer

He didn't steal their money. He didn't steal their cities or towns. He stole their hearts. If a man or woman's heart be stolen then they will be deeply influenced by the thief and Absalom was an expert heart-stealer.

'Whenever anyone came near him to bow down ... he would put out his hand and take him and kiss him'.

David's son was a smooth operator: slick, silver-tongued and handsome. *'In all Israel there was no one who was praised so much for his good looks, from the sole of his foot to the crown of his head there was no blemish in him.'* When such a character starts talking, people listen and it was not long before his winsome ways had stolen a nation of hearts.

He was also a very vain man. *'When he cut the hair of his head'* (at the end of every year he cut it because it was very heavy on him), he weighed the hair of his head at about *2.3 kilograms* according to the King's standard.

His public relations exercise in Israel was not only to greet and win the favour of everyone who came to his father with a problem, but he knew how easily folks were impressed with outward appearances.

He got himself horses and chariots and 50 men to run before him. People by the million, in all ages fall for the old trick that, 'The medium is the message.'

That the man had treason in his heart and could not wait for God's time for him to have a position of influence in the land, never dawned on them. That a man's life does not consist of the abundance of things he possesses did not occur to them. That a hypocrite preaches by the yard but practices by the inch was hidden to the nation by 'Just-look-at-all-those-chariots-and-footmen.'

Absalom was in a hurry and God was not even in his reckoning. Absalom led a rebellion against his father when Shimei cursed David and threw stones at him as David fled Jerusalem saying, *'The Lord has delivered the Kingdom into the hands of Absalom your son so now you are caught'* the heart-stealer seemed to have God on his side.

God, however, is the great *heart-searcher*. God is not always in the whirlwind, the earthquake or the fire. He sometimes speaks in the still, small voice.

David must have meditated on the grace of God on that lonely hillside because his words reflect it. *'It may be that the Lord will look on my affliction and that the Lord will repay me with good for his cursing this day.'*

He did just that for Absalom soon swung from a tree, caught by his long hair in the thick boughs of an oak, speared through the heart. Taken and cast into a pit and covered with a very large heap of stones, Absalom is a monument of warning to all of us not to be taken in by what seems great.

God does not ask primarily for our money, our home, or land, our hands or our feet. 'My son, give me your heart,' he whispers. Let him have that and he has all. Let any other false king reign in your hearts and we will be, as Israel found to their cost, disillusioned.